First Facts™

Holidays and Culture

Hanukkah

Jewish Festival of Lights

by Terri Sievert

Consultant:
Rabbi Kerry M. Olitzky
Executive Director, Jewish Outreach Institute
New York, New York

Capstone
press
Mankato, Minnesota

First Facts is published by Capstone Press,
151 Good Counsel Drive, P.O. Box 669, Mankato, Minnesota 56002.
www.capstonepress.com

Library of Congress Cataloging-in-Publication Data
Sievert, Terri.
    Hanukkah : Jewish festival of lights / by Terri Sievert.
       p. cm.—(First facts. Holidays and culture)
    Summary: "A brief description of what Hanukkah is, how it started, and ways people
celebrate this cultural holiday"—Provided by publisher.
    Includes bibliographical references and index.
    ISBN-13: 978-0-7368-5389-7 (hardcover)
    ISBN-10: 0-7368-5389-8 (hardcover)
    1. Hanukkah—Juvenile literature. I. Title. II. Series.
BM695.H3S467 2006
296.4'35—dc22   2005015589

4751

Editorial Credits
Jennifer Besel, editor; Juliette Peters, designer; Wanda Winch, photo researcher; Scott Thoms,
    photo editor

Photo Credits
The Billings Gazette/Steve Smith, 20
Capstone Press/Karon Dubke, cover, 18, 21
Comstock, 1
The Granger Collection, New York, 9, 10–11, 12–13
Photodisc/David Buffington, 14
PhotoEdit Inc./Bill Aron, 17, 19; Richard Hutchings, 15
Photri-MicroStock/Richard Nowitz, 5
SuperStock/Kwame Zikomo, 6

1 2 3 4 5 6 11 10 09 08 07 06

Table of Contents

Celebrating Hanukkah

Candles flicker in a special **menorah**. Family members gather around the glowing lights. They smile and sing prayers for Hanukkah.

Each year, **Jews** celebrate Hanukkah for eight nights in November or December. Hanukkah brightens the darkest time of year.

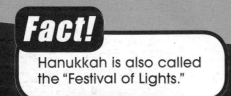

Fact!
Hanukkah is also called the "Festival of Lights."

What Is Hanukkah?

Hanukkah is a Jewish holiday. During Hanukkah, Jews honor their **culture.** They celebrate their faith and way of life.

Hanukkah is a time for families to gather together. They talk about their Jewish history and a **miracle** that happened in a **temple** long ago.

Fact!
The word Hanukkah means "dedication."

Starting a War

The history of Hanukkah goes back thousands of years. The Jews lived in a country called Judea, but they were ruled by a king from another country. The king wanted the Jews to change their religion and pray to his Greek gods. But the Jews refused to **worship** anything but their own God. So the angry king sent his army to attack the Jewish people.

Fact!

The Jews fought for their faith in Judea. Today, this country is called Israel.

9

10

Victory

A man named Judah led the Jews' fight against the king's army. Judah was called Maccabee, which means "the hammer." His followers were called the Maccabees.

After three years, the Maccabees beat the king's army. They had finally won the freedom to live as they wanted.

The Miracle

The Jews gathered to pray in their temple once again. They had only enough oil to light the menorah for one day. But by a miracle, it burned for eight days.

Hanukkah reminds Jews of their struggle to worship freely. They think about how their faith helped them get through very hard times.

Fact!
The miracle of Hanukkah is written in a holy book called the Talmud.

12

Hanukkah Candles

Families remember the miracle by lighting candles for eight nights. A Hanukkah menorah holds nine candles. Eight candles stand for the eight nights the oil burned.

The ninth candle is the *shammash* (SHAM-mash). Family members take turns using the *shammash* to light the other candles.

Hanukkah Food

Many Hanukkah foods are fried in oil. The oily taste reminds people of the oil that burned for eight days.

During Hanukkah, many families make latkes (LAHT-kuhs). These pancakes are made with potatoes and onions. Fried doughnuts filled with jelly are a special Hanukkah treat.

Fact!

Some people believe the Maccabees ate pancakes made from cheese, fruit, or vegetables. Eating potato latkes is a special custom that reminds Jews of their history.

Gifts and Games

Gifts are an exciting part of Hanukkah. Each night, family members give each other presents. Money, called gelt, is a traditional gift.

The **dreidel** game celebrates the Hanukkah miracle. Children spin a top to win prizes. Symbols painted on the toy remind children of their Jewish history.

The dreidel symbols are Hebrew letters. They stand for the phrase "a great miracle happened there."

שׁ = shin

ה = hei

ג = gimel

נ = nun

19

Amazing Holiday Story!

In 1993, a Jewish family in Montana lit a menorah for Hanukkah. Suddenly, someone sent a brick crashing through their window.

This act was meant to scare all Jewish families. Instead, it made people in the town come together to support the holiday. Although many were not Jewish, people placed paper menorahs in their own windows. At least 10,000 menorahs were proudly displayed to support the Jewish holiday.

Hands On: Milk Carton Dreidel

Dreidel is a fun game to play with friends. You can make your own Hanukkah dreidel.

What You Need

stapler

small milk carton
(rinsed and dried)

dark blue paint

small paint brush

gold glitter pen

sharpened pencil

bag of chocolate coins

What You Do

1. Staple the spout of the milk carton closed.
2. Paint the carton with the blue paint, so none of the print shows through. Let it dry.
3. With the glitter pen, draw one Hebrew letter on each side of the milk carton. (See the chart on page 19 for the letters.)
4. When the glitter is dry, poke the pencil through the carton.
5. To play the game, get together with two or three friends. Divide the chocolate coins evenly between all players. Have everyone put one coin into a pile. Take turns spinning the dreidel. When *shin* faces up, the spinner puts another coin in the pile. When *nun* faces up, do nothing. *Hei* means the spinner wins half the candy in the pile. *Gimel* means the spinner wins everything in the pile! Then the game starts over.

Glossary

culture (KUHL-chur)—a people's way of life, ideas, art, customs, and traditions

dreidel (DRAY-duhl)—a toy spun like a top in a game of chance

Jew (JOO)—a person who practices the religion of Judaism; Judaism is based on a belief in one God and the teachings of a holy book called the Torah.

menorah (muh-NOR-uh)—a candleholder used in the Jewish religion

miracle (MIHR-uh-kuhl)—an amazing event that can't be explained by the laws of nature

temple (TEM-puhl)—a Jewish place of worship

worship (WUR-ship)—to express love or honor to a higher being

Read More

Erlbach, Arlene. *Hanukkah: Celebrating the Holiday of Lights.* Finding Out About Holidays. Berkeley Heights, N.J.: Enslow, 2001.

Fishman, Cathy Goldberg. *Hanukkah.* On My Own Holidays. Minneapolis: Carolrhoda Books, 2004.

Internet Sites

FactHound offers a safe, fun way to find Internet sites related to this book. All of the sites on FactHound have been researched by our staff.

Here's how:
1. Visit *www.facthound.com*
2. Type in this special code **0736853898** for age-appropriate sites. Or enter a search word related to this book for a more general search.
3. Click on the **Fetch It** button.

FactHound will fetch the best sites for you!

Index